Cambridge English Readers
· ·
Level 4

Series editor: Philip Prowse

Staying Together

Judith Wilson

CAMBRIDGE
UNIVERSITY PRESS

PUBLISHED BY THE PRESS SYNDICATE OF THE UNIVERSITY OF CAMBRIDGE
The Pitt Building, Trumpington Street, Cambridge, United Kingdom

CAMBRIDGE UNIVERSITY PRESS
The Edinburgh Building, Cambridge CB2 2RU, UK
40 West 20th Street, New York, NY 10011-4211, USA
477 Williamstown Road, Port Melbourne, VIC 3207, Australia
Ruiz de Alarcón 13, 28014 Madrid, Spain
Dock House, The Waterfront, Cape Town 8001, South Africa

http://www.cambridge.org

First published 2001
Fourth printing 2004

Printed in India by Thomson Press Limited

Typeset in 12/15pt Adobe Garamond [CE]

ISBN 0 521 79848 5   paperback
ISBN 0 521 79849 3   cassette

Contents

Characters

Ikuko Kanazawa: an office worker in Tokyo.
Hiroshi Masuda: Ikuko's boyfriend.
Bernard Chiluba: an African student.
Lucretia: a Brazilian student.
Mike: a photography teacher.
Joyce Mutanga: a media-scientist.
Fatima: head of the Red Sea Research Centre.
Taka: a researcher at the Centre.
Sven: a researcher at the Centre.

ENGLAND
○ Birmingham
● Broadway
London ○

JAPAN
Ome ○
● Tokyo
Ryūkyū Islands

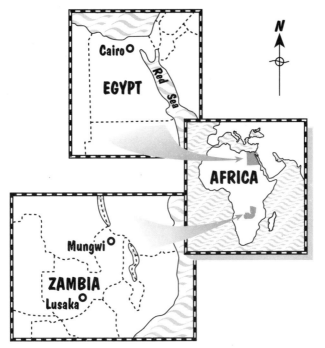

N

Cairo ○
Red Sea
EGYPT

AFRICA

Mungwi ○
ZAMBIA
Lusaka ○

Part 1 Going away

Chapter 1 *The promise*

'Are we really eating here, Hiroshi?' Ikuko stopped by the door of the expensive Tokyo restaurant, looking unsure.

Hiroshi smiled as he held the door open for her. 'Of course. It's your birthday. Everything's arranged.'

Inside, the big room was almost full. Well-dressed people talked softly together. The waiter showed Ikuko and Hiroshi to their table and brought them a bottle of wine. Ikuko felt a little nervous. This wasn't the sort of place they usually came to. But when Hiroshi smiled at her across the table, with his dark hair falling into his eyes as usual, she felt better.

Hiroshi raised his glass. 'Happy birthday, Ikuko,' he said. 'How does it feel to be twenty-three?'

She smiled. 'I can't believe it. I still feel sixteen.'

As they came to the end of their meal, they fell silent and looked at one another. There was a candle burning on the table and Ikuko could see its light in Hiroshi's eyes. After a moment Hiroshi put his hand in the pocket of his jacket, and brought out a little box.

'Ikuko,' he said, and then stopped. 'Ikuko, you know how I feel about you. I've never met anyone else like you. I'd like you to have this. I'd like us to stay together always.'

He handed the box across the table to Ikuko. She opened

it, her hands shaking. Inside there was a ring. It was a simple ring, perfectly chosen for her by someone who loved her. But part of her was thinking, 'This isn't happening to me.' It was as if she was watching someone in a movie.

She knew her parents liked Hiroshi. He was a considerate man who had done well in his company and would look after Ikuko, their only daughter. Her friends liked him too – he was kind and always ready to help anyone with a problem. Ikuko knew that she liked being with Hiroshi and that he'd never made her feel unhappy for a moment. She couldn't imagine her life without him. So why did the idea of marrying him seem like a door closing on the future?

Hiroshi put his hand on hers. Ikuko looked up at him. 'Hiroshi. I do love you. But ... if we get married now, what will I do then?'

'I'll look after you. You won't need to work any more. You'll have time to do all the things you want to do.' Hiroshi spoke with his usual optimism. 'You can carry on with your English classes and do more of the things you enjoy ... things like your photography. We can get a flat – maybe even a house one day, with a garden for the children.'

'It sounds lovely,' replied Ikuko. 'But I'm younger than you. I've never really done anything. I just went straight into the Hayakawa company after college. You've done lots of things – you've travelled and studied in America. You've learnt something about the world.'

'Ikuko, people talk about travelling as such a great thing, but what I found is that I like Japan best. I had American friends, sure, but we never got very close. You can never really understand someone from another culture. Believe me, the most beautiful places and the people who matter most are the ones in your own country, your own home.'

Ikuko thought she'd be happy with Hiroshi. She'd imagined spending her life with him – just not so soon. She knew she would have to tell him how she felt. But before she could find the words, Hiroshi found them for her.

'Ikuko, I remember how much I once wanted to travel. And I don't want you to miss that chance if it's what you really want. So if you want to go and study for a few months, in America or in England, I can wait for you.'

'He understands so well,' thought Ikuko. Suddenly, everything seemed clear.

'Yes,' she said at last. 'I think I need a few months to see things for myself. To grow up a little more. Will you wait for me? Then I'll come back and we can get married.'

'Don't grow up too much, Ikuko. I like you just as you are,' said Hiroshi. Gently he put the ring onto her finger.

*   *   *

Two months later, Ikuko turned off her computer in the big office in the Hayakawa building for the last time. Outside, the Tokyo sky was dark and lights were already shining in the tall office buildings. She got up from her desk and went across the room, past the desk of old Mr Honma, the office manager. He looked up as she walked past. 'Well, Ikuko, so it's goodbye. We'll miss you. Where are you going to in England, anyway? London?'

'No – a place called Birmingham,' Ikuko replied.

'Never heard of it. Is it beautiful there?' he asked.

'I don't know. But I'll bring lots of photos back.'

She went to get her jacket. It was a cold December day and she pulled on a warm hat in front of the mirror. She looked at herself. The girl looking back at her out of the mirror did not look very different from the girl who had started work there more than two years before: a pale serious face with long straight hair and a pointed chin. She wondered how this next year would change her – living in England, and then the wedding.

On the train journey home, Ikuko sat and thought about the past two years. She'd been lucky to get the job in the Hayakawa company. Lucky because it was a good company and she found the work interesting. And lucky because she'd met Hiroshi there.

She remembered the day they'd met. It had been late on a Friday afternoon. She'd only been working there for a few weeks and she was still feeling unsure of herself. She was entering numbers on the computer for a sales program. But the results looked wrong. She took a deep breath and went up to Mr Honma's desk to tell him. Mr Honma hadn't been very helpful, but he'd arranged for one of the programmers to have a look.

Half an hour later Ikuko had looked up to see a tall man, young and with rather untidy hair, coming across the room towards her. He stopped and introduced himself.

'I'm Hiroshi Masuda. I hear you have some problems with the sales program,' he said.

Ikuko explained and Hiroshi listened carefully, then sat down and did some work on the computer. Suddenly he stopped and looked up at her, brushing his hair out of his eyes. He was excited. 'You're absolutely right. There's a mistake in the program. I knew there was something wrong with the numbers we were getting. Now we can change it. Thanks!' He stood up. 'Anyway, it's probably time you got off home. Do you live far away?'

'In Ome. It's an hour away on the train,' said Ikuko.

'Oh, yes, I know. In fact I go through Ome on my way home. So we've been travelling on the same train. I'm surprised we haven't seen one another before.'

'Well, the trains are so crowded,' Ikuko said.

'Yes,' he said, 'but I'd notice you, even in a crowd.'

And that was how it had begun. Sitting in the train now, two years later, Ikuko remembered the early days of their friendship: meals in small restaurants, walks in the park – slowly getting to know each other. They discovered that they'd both gone to the same Junior High school, although Hiroshi had been four years ahead of Ikuko. After leaving university, he'd gone to do a computing course in America. He'd done very well, but hadn't enjoyed life in America and decided instead to return to Tokyo.

In those first days of new love, Ikuko and Hiroshi had spent almost all their free time together. Ikuko liked his gentleness and understanding. It was the perfect relationship. No arguments or bad surprises. Wasn't that what she wanted?

'Ome . . . Ome.' Ikuko heard the name of her station and woke suddenly from her thoughts. She got off and walked out of the crowded station. On her way home, she stopped at a department store – she still had to buy a suitcase for her trip. As she walked to the suitcase department, she passed a shelf of diaries. She stopped. That wasn't what she'd come for. She looked at the diaries a moment longer and then chose one with a plain white cover.

In the suitcase department, she quickly found what she was looking for.

'I'll take that one,' she said, pointing to a blue suitcase. It was expensive, but she was going a long way. And she could use it for her honeymoon later on.

*   *   *

A few days later Ikuko was sitting in Narita International Airport with Hiroshi. The blue suitcase had already been checked in on the London flight, and they were having one last coffee together.

The two of them had hardly spoken on the way to the airport. Ikuko wondered if she was making a terrible mistake. 'It's only for six months,' she said to Hiroshi, trying to persuade herself as much as him.

'A lot can happen in six months,' he said. 'I don't want to lose you. Remember you promised to come back.'

Ikuko looked at her ring. 'I'll come back,' she said.

They said goodbye, but as she went through to the departure lounge she looked back one last time. Hiroshi was still standing there, his hair falling into his eyes, looking lost and lonely in the middle of the airport crowds.

Chapter 2   *The blue suitcase*

'Can you describe the suitcase?' asked the woman at the desk in Heathrow Airport. Ikuko felt like crying. It had been a bad flight. She'd been sitting next to two children who were noisy and who couldn't sit still. Ikuko hadn't been able to sleep at all. And now her suitcase was lost. With her clothes, her camera – everything.

She said slowly in English, 'It was blue ... '

The woman smiled at her kindly. 'Don't worry. Just fill in this form. I'm sure we'll find it. It will probably be on the next plane. We'll send it on.'

Slowly Ikuko wrote a description of the suitcase and what was in it, and the address she would be staying at: Selly Park Hostel, Oak Road, Selly Oak, Birmingham.

Four long hours later the taxi drove up in front of a big old house with trees around it. It was seven o'clock. It had been a long, difficult journey from Heathrow Airport – the London underground, the train to Birmingham and the taxi from the station to the hostel.

Ikuko walked up to the hostel. She thought the building looked like pictures of churches she'd seen with its dark stone walls and pointed windows. Two students came out of the door, talking in a language Ikuko didn't understand. She went inside. There was no-one at the reception desk, but there was a sign: 'Ring bell for service'. She rang it.

After a moment a door opened and a woman came out. 'Can I help you?'

'I'm Ikuko ... Ikuko Kanazawa.'

'Oh, yes. We were expecting you. You're in room 31. Come along, I'll show you. Where's your suitcase?'

Ikuko started to tell her, but the woman didn't seem to be listening.

'Oh dear. Never mind,' she said. 'Now, here's your room. Dinner's finished now, but there are plenty of restaurants five minutes away on Bristol Road if you want something to eat. Breakfast's at eight – back in the main building, on the ground floor. OK? Do you understand?'

'Yes,' Ikuko said as the door closed, leaving her alone. But she wasn't sure she had understood. The woman sounded different from the recordings she'd listened to in her English lessons. Maybe it was because Ikuko was so tired.

She looked around the room: a bed, a desk, a lamp. She wanted a bath, but she had no towel. She wasn't hungry, and anyway she couldn't face going out into the cold strange streets that night. She wanted to ring Hiroshi – but in Japan it would be four o'clock in the morning.

The room felt cold and she got into bed to try to keep warm. She was tired but her mind was still active. She took her new diary out of her handbag and started to write in English.

9 January 2000
Today I arrived in England. It's very exciting.

She thought for a moment. 'Who am I writing this for?' she wondered. 'Will I show it to Hiroshi? Or is it just for me? Anyway, I should write the truth.' She started again.

Today I arrived in England. My suitcase is lost. The journey was quite difficult. I'm disappointed that I can't understand English people better. Now I'm in my room in the student hostel. I feel so lonely. I miss Hiroshi. Maybe he was right about travelling.

She put down her pen feeling close to tears. This was not how she had expected to feel on her first day in England. She put her head down on her pillow – maybe if she had a rest she'd feel better . . .

*   *   *

There was a knock on the door and a man's voice. 'Ikuko Kanazawa?'

The room was dark and for a minute Ikuko didn't know where she was. She turned on the light and looked at her watch. It was seven o'clock on Monday morning and she was in England.

There was another knock, and then footsteps going away. Ikuko got out of bed and realised she was still wearing all her clothes. She felt hot and uncomfortable.

She went to the door and opened it. A man was disappearing down the corridor. She could only see his back – black hair and a red jacket. And in front of the door was her blue suitcase.

Chapter 3 *The first week*

Ikuko carried the suitcase into her room, feeling much better. Now she could have a shower and change her clothes. But first she must ring Hiroshi. She got her mobile phone out of her handbag and dialled his number.

'So what's Birmingham like?' he asked, sounding very far away. He'd never understood why she'd wanted to study in Birmingham and not somewhere more famous like Oxford or Cambridge. But she hadn't wanted to stay in a tourist centre, even if it was beautiful. She'd wanted to see how English people really lived.

But now she wasn't so sure. She walked over to the window of her small bedroom and looked out. There was a narrow road with cars parked along it, and a few trees with no leaves left on them. Everything looked cold and dark in the early morning light.

'Well,' she said, 'it's sort of grey.'

An hour later, Ikuko found the dining room of the hostel. She walked in shyly. There was a smell of fried food and a sound of quiet talking. She looked around and saw that, although there were some people in groups, quite a few people were sitting alone. 'Maybe I'm not the only person who's just arrived,' she thought.

A large woman came over and said, 'Are you new here, dear? Do you want a cooked breakfast?'

Ikuko looked confused. What was a cooked breakfast? But the woman became impatient. 'Bacon and eggs?' she said loudly.

'Yes ... yes, please,' Ikuko replied.

As she sat alone eating, Ikuko wondered if any of the students in the room were English. She could see a group of Japanese students – a boy with bright yellow hair and earrings, and two girls dressed in tight fashionable clothes. Nearer to her was a group of girls talking in English and another language. Everyone looked very young.

'Will I have anything in common with these people?' she thought. 'Maybe I should just get a flight back to Japan.'

She took a deep breath. She'd got her suitcase. Things weren't so bad. Time to go to her English class. She finished her breakfast and walked out of the room.

Ten minutes later she walked out into the street. She took out the map she'd been given with directions to the language centre and started to walk. She was supposed to get a bus, but where was the bus stop? She tried to work it out from her map.

Then someone spoke to her in Japanese. 'Are you going to the language centre?'

She turned round. It was the Japanese boy with yellow hair. He was with two other students, a dark-haired girl and a taller boy.

'Yes ... yes,' she said to the Japanese boy. 'On the 65 bus?'

'That's right.' Then he continued in English, 'Come with us. We're all going, too.'

And sitting in the pub that evening with a glass of warm beer in front of her which took her all evening to finish,

Ikuko realised she already had friends. Sitting opposite her was the Japanese boy with yellow hair. His name was Toshi. 'Everyone calls me crazy Toshi,' he said, laughing. He'd been in England for a long time and seemed to know everyone. Next to him was Pietro from Italy. And sitting next to Ikuko was Lucretia, the dark-haired girl who had been with Toshi that morning. She was from South America. From a town called Recife, in Brazil. Lucretia had shown her where it was on the map in the classroom.

Ikuko liked Lucretia's warm smile, her green eyes and her confident English. She talked so quickly that Ikuko could hardly follow.

'Oh, yes,' said Lucretia, as they sat talking in the pub. 'But my writing! No good at all! I have to improve.'

'How long have you been here?' asked Ikuko.

'Three months. I need to pass my IELTS exam, then I can do Business Studies at the University.'

Later, they all walked back to the hostel together through the dark streets.

'Who wants some good Italian coffee?' asked Pietro. But suddenly all Ikuko wanted was to be on her own. She said good night to them and went to her room. But before she went to sleep she got out her diary.

10 January 2000

What a long day ... so many things happened. My suitcase arrived. I went to my first English class and made some friends from different countries. It's very hard speaking in English all day. Everyone's friendly, but they're all a bit younger than me. I like Lucretia, she's very lively, and kind, too. We went to the pub. It was hard to understand people, it was so noisy.

Everyone seemed to be having a good time, though. But it's not quite what I expected. What did I expect, really? I don't know.

*   *   *

As she sat in the coffee bar waiting for Lucretia on Friday afternoon, Ikuko couldn't believe that she'd only been in England for five days. It seemed much longer. She already felt at home in the hostel and was getting to know the tree-lined streets of her little corner of Birmingham.

She wandered over to the notice board on the wall of the coffee bar. Among the notices for discos and films there was one which caught her attention.

Photography club.
Next meeting: Saturday 15 January at 2pm. Room 261.
Pictures of people – Bernard Chiluba
All welcome.

She thought of her camera lying unused on the desk in her room. She used to belong to a photography club in Junior High school. It would be nice to learn a little bit more about photography – and to take some pictures to show Hiroshi. Saturday afternoon. That was tomorrow. She wrote down the place and time.

Just then Lucretia came up behind her. 'Oh, photography. That's supposed to be a good club. But Saturdays are for shopping. Don't you want to go into town instead?'

'Thanks, but I don't like shopping much,' replied Ikuko.

18

'No?' said Lucretia, looking surprised. 'Funny, I love shopping. OK, well call round to my room about five o'clock. I'll show you what I've bought.'

*   *   *

At two o'clock the next day Ikuko shyly opened the door of room 261. It was a small room full of people talking to one another. She didn't know anyone there, but a young man with curly brown hair and glasses came over to her.

'Hi. Welcome. Have you come to join the club?'

'Yes . . . I think so,' said Ikuko.

'Great. I'm Mike. I'm the one who started the club. And you're . . . ?'

'Ikuko. What do you do in the club?'

'Well, it's really just a chance to get together and help one another,' Mike explained. 'We've got a darkroom, so you can develop your pictures here if you want . . . '

'Develop?' Ikuko didn't understand.

'Yes, instead of taking the film to a photo shop, you can learn to do it yourself – just black and white though, not colour. And we go out together, taking pictures. Usually just in Birmingham, but sometimes we go to the country.'

He spoke quickly, but Ikuko managed to understand. She was pleased. Except for her teachers, she hadn't really spoken to many English people.

'Have you done much photography in . . . Japan, is it?' asked Mike.

'Just a little. But I'd like to learn a bit more,' Ikuko replied.

'Well, today Bernard's going to show us some of the pictures he's taken of people in Birmingham. Bernard Chiluba, over there.' Mike pointed at a tall man standing with his back to them – black hair, very short and curly, and a red jacket. Where had she seen that jacket before?

Hearing his name, the man turned round and came up to them. His skin was very dark brown, almost black, smooth and shining. He seemed a little older than the other students.

'Bernard, this is Ikuko,' said Mike.

Bernard smiled, a wide smile, his teeth very white in his dark face. Ikuko noticed that his smile was crooked, a little wider on one side than the other. He held out his hand and she shook it, still looking at him.

'Hello, Ikuko.'

His hand held hers powerfully. His voice was deep and she liked the soft slow way he said her name. He continued talking: 'But I think we're neighbours. Are you Ikuko with the blue suitcase?'

And then Ikuko remembered the red jacket she'd seen disappearing down the corridor on the first morning.

She let go of his hand, feeling suddenly shy. 'Oh ... thank you ... yes, it was my suitcase. How ... how did you know it was mine?'

'I was just leaving the hostel when it arrived from the airport. It was early in the morning. The receptionist was busy – so I said I'd take it up for her.'

'Oh, thank you ... that was very kind.' She noticed how clearly he spoke. Not too fast like all the other people she'd met, not hurrying on before she had time to reply.

'So you're from Japan?' he asked.

'Yes . . . and you?'

'I'm from Zambia. In Africa.'

Around them people were starting to sit down. 'Right, excuse us, Ikuko,' said Mike, and he went up to the front and introduced Bernard's talk. Ikuko listened to Bernard's deep voice explaining the pictures. She had never seen any like them before. He had taken them all in Birmingham, but the people in them seemed to come from every corner of the world: Jamaica, Pakistan, China. Ikuko wondered if she could ever learn to make silent faces come alive like that.

At the end of the meeting she went up to Bernard. 'Thank you. They're wonderful pictures.'

Bernard smiled at her. 'Thanks. It's something I really enjoy doing.' He looked at her a little uncertainly. 'We're just going for coffee. Would you like to come?'

Ikuko looked at her watch. It was half past four. She remembered that she was meeting Lucretia back at the hostel. 'No . . . I'm sorry, I can't. I have to meet someone.'

'Oh, OK,' he said and turned away.

Chapter 4 *City centre*

The next Saturday Ikuko woke up early. She looked out of her window and saw the sun for almost the first time, shining on the trees in the garden next door. What a beautiful morning! 'A whole day free,' she thought. 'I really should be a bit braver. I've not really seen anything of Birmingham yet.' She decided to go and explore.

An hour later she was waiting for the bus. When it arrived she asked for a ticket to the town centre and sat down in an empty seat near the front. The doors closed, but there was the sound of running steps and the doors opened again to let one more person on. Ikuko saw a red jacket and recognised the deep voice speaking to the driver. 'Thank you. City centre, please.'

He had almost walked past Ikuko when she suddenly heard herself say, 'Bernard?'

He looked up, surprised. 'Oh, Ikuko. I didn't see you,' he said as he sat down next to her. She could feel him very close in the narrow bus seat. They were quiet for a moment, then they both started talking at the same time.

'Are you . . . '

'I haven't seen you . . . '

They laughed. 'Go on,' said Bernard.

'I haven't seen you . . . are you still staying in the hostel?'

'Sure. But I get up earlier than most people. I'm usually the first person at breakfast.'

'You're not studying at the language centre, are you?'

'No, I'm in the Department of Education. I'm doing a teaching diploma. So I'm over at the university most of the day – and I eat at the university in the evenings, too.'

'Is your course difficult?' she asked him.

'Yes, there's a lot of work. But I'm used to hard work. At home I'm a teacher already. But I got a scholarship from the government to pay to come here and do the diploma.'

She wondered what his life was like, back in Zambia. 'Do you live in the capital?' she asked.

'No. I come from the north of Zambia, a small town called Mungwi. There's just a school and a few shops. We don't even have a hospital. No big buildings at all. Not like Birmingham.' He smiled, the crooked smile she'd noticed before. 'And what are you going to do in Birmingham this morning? Are you going shopping?'

'No,' Ikuko replied. 'I just wanted to have a look at Birmingham.'

'It's a fine city. I like it,' he said. 'Lots of people complain about it. But it's alive. It's always growing, always changing.'

Around them now were tall buildings shining in the sun. Then the bus went down a narrow street and stopped.

'This is where we get off.' They followed the other passengers off the bus. Then Bernard turned to her. 'If you want ... I could show you a bit of Birmingham.'

'Yes, please,' said Ikuko. 'I'd like that a lot.'

They walked together through the centre of Birmingham, in the middle of the Saturday crowds. Bernard showed her the little cathedral in its tiny green garden, the art gallery, and the new shops and restaurants built where the old factories had once stood. They talked about what they saw, about Birmingham and their own countries. Ikuko hardly noticed her tired feet or the cold wind.

Then Bernard looked at his watch. 'It's lunchtime. It's after one o'clock. What do you want to do?'

'Shall we go to a restaurant?' she suggested. 'Or we could go back to the hostel?'

'I can't face hostel food,' said Bernard. 'Let's go to an Indian restaurant. I know a good one near here.'

The restaurant was small, but warm and friendly. The Indian waiter was pleased to see them. 'Hi, Bernard. You all right, then? Where's your camera?'

'You've seen him before,' said Bernard to Ikuko. 'In one of the photos.' He showed her how to eat the spicy meat with pieces of bread in her fingers. 'This is how we eat at home; we don't use knives and forks. The food tastes better like this. But in Zambia we mostly eat *nshima* instead of bread or potatoes. Oh, I miss *nshima*!'

'Yes, I miss rice. They have rice in the hostel but it's different from the rice in Japan. It's hard,' said Ikuko.

'And in Japan you eat with those sticks, don't you?'

'Chopsticks? Yes, it's easy. I'll show you! But we don't use them all the time – sometimes we eat the western way.'

'Do you live with your family?' he asked. It was the first personal question he'd asked her.

'Yes.' She wondered if she should tell him about Hiroshi. But it didn't seem the right moment. Bernard was quiet for a moment, too. She wondered if he was thinking of his home. 'How about you?' she asked. 'Do you live with your parents?'

'No, my parents are very old. They live alone ... ' He looked as if he was going to say something more but then was silent again.

Ikuko felt this was not something he wanted to talk about. She waited a minute then changed the subject. 'How long have you been taking photos?'

'Oh, a long time. It's always been my hobby. But I'm starting a photography business of my own,' he said.

'As well as teaching?' Ikuko asked.

'Yes. It'll be hard work, but I can do it. People always want photographs. They need them for their passports and other papers, and they want them for special times too – weddings and other ceremonies. There's no photographer in Mungwi, so if I can develop my own pictures it will mean I can earn more money. How about you, Ikuko? Do you have a job in Japan?'

'No, not any more,' she answered. 'I left my job.'

'So what will you do when you go back to Japan?'

Ikuko looked at the ring on her finger. 'I don't know exactly,' she said. 'There's someone ... '

'I see,' said Bernard. 'I understand.'

22 January 2000

Today I spent the morning in Birmingham with Bernard. He showed me so many things. And tonight he's invited me to meet his friends. We're going to listen to Zambian music and eat Zambian food. I hope we can be good friends. He's different from anyone else I've met here. Different from anyone I've ever met.

Chapter 5 *Snowfall*

'So you're off with Bernard again this weekend?' It was Saturday morning and Lucretia was sitting in Ikuko's room, drinking coffee. She looked at Ikuko over the top of her coffee cup.

'It's just the photography club. We're going to the country. To a place called Broadway,' Ikuko replied.

Lucretia raised her eyebrows, but didn't say anything. Ikuko knew what she was thinking.

'We're just friends, Lucretia. Really. He knows there's someone in Japan.'

'But, Ikuko, does that someone in Japan know about Bernard?' Lucretia asked.

'It's not like that,' Ikuko began. 'Bernard and I ... In some ways we're very close. We like the same things. But we don't talk about him and me and things like that.' She looked at her ring. 'I haven't said anything to Hiroshi. I don't want to worry him ... about nothing.'

'But is it nothing?' asked Lucretia. 'Because sometimes when I see you two together, it seems as if there's more.'

'No, there's no more. We go for walks. We talk a lot. I'm finding out about so many different places and people ... about Africa, about Zambia: the stories, the music. I'm learning how to dance.' Ikuko remembered the feel of Bernard's hand in hers as they danced together.

When Ikuko was with Bernard, everything seemed fine. So why did she feel so confused?

'Be careful, Ikuko.'

'I'll be all right, Lucretia. Really.'

*   *   *

'OK everyone, let's go!' Mike started up the minibus and they drove off through the grey streets, then along the motorway and into the countryside. Ikuko and Bernard looked out of the window at the frozen fields and cloudy sky. Ikuko realised that she was turning her ring round and round on her finger. Bernard was unusually quiet, too. They turned off the motorway and slowed down as the road got narrower and the hills got steeper. Soon they came into a village and the minibus stopped by the side of the street.

'Right, everyone, we're here,' said Mike as he came round and opened the side door. 'I hope you've all got warm clothes on – it's freezing! I suggest we have a look round the village and take any pictures before the light goes. Then meet back at the tea-rooms here at four o'clock.'

The cold wind hit them as they got off the bus. They were in the middle of a street with small old houses on both sides. Although it was only two o'clock, the houses all had lights on. They walked along together, heads down against the cold. Some of the group stopped and went into the little shops, but Mike, Ikuko and Bernard carried on until they reached an old church. They walked down the path to the church door. On either side of the path, there were grey tombstones with the names of people who had died and been laid there under the ground hundreds of years ago. There were small white flowers among the tombstones.

'What are they called?' asked Ikuko.

'They're snowdrops – the first spring flowers,' said Mike.

Ikuko bent down with her camera, trying to take a picture of the small flowers, but it was already too dark. A few flakes of snow started to fall.

'Snow,' said Bernard. 'So this is what it looks like. I've never seen it before.' He turned to Ikuko, smiling.

'Let's go inside the church,' said Mike.

Inside it smelt of stone and candles. They walked around quietly.

'Ikuko, look.' Bernard showed her an old tombstone. There was a stone woman on it, lying with her hands crossed. Ikuko looked at it, wondering about the woman's life. She looked young – about the same age as Ikuko. Suddenly, a flash lit the darkness and Ikuko looked up in surprise. Bernard stood there with his camera. 'You looked lovely standing there, as if you were made of stone yourself,' he said.

When they came out of the church it was snowing harder and the ground was already white.

'Let's try to get some pictures of it,' said Bernard.

But Mike was worried. 'I don't like this,' he said. 'We'd better get back.' They hurried back to the tea-room and found the others there already. Ikuko wanted to stay and get warm but there was no time.

'Sorry,' said Mike. 'But it's a bad road until we get to the motorway. We need to leave as soon as possible.'

They got back into the minibus. Ikuko and Bernard were sitting near the front with Bernard next to the window. Mike got into the driver's seat and set off, driving slowly and carefully. Everyone was quiet. The minibus started to go up a hill, very slowly.

Suddenly there were lights in front of them, then a bang that seemed to go right through Ikuko. She heard screams and felt herself being thrown towards the front window. There was a sound of breaking glass.

A second later Ikuko was lying across the minibus seat, almost on the floor. Bernard had his arms tightly round her.

'Bernard . . . ?'

'Yes . . . are you OK?'

'I think so.' She pulled herself up carefully. At the back of the bus people were shouting. But at the front everything was quiet. She got up and moved towards the driver's seat. The engine was still running but Mike was not moving. He lay face down in his seat, his hair covered in broken glass, the wet snow blowing in through the broken window.

Ikuko stretched over and turned off the engine. She could hear voices now outside. The driver of the other vehicle – a van – had got out and was talking to the other students. She could just see them, dark against the snow.

She bent over Mike and gently lifted up his face, frightened of what she might find. Bernard came up behind her and she turned to him. 'He's breathing,' she said. 'We need to get help for him. My mobile phone . . . It's in my bag – probably on the floor somewhere. Can you get it?'

A minute later, Bernard came back with the phone. But she realised she didn't know what number to ring, who to ask for or what to say. She gave it to Bernard. The people outside kept on talking. Suddenly there seemed to be nothing to do except wait, as the snow continued to fall.

Much later that night, the two of them went back to the hostel together. They were both very quiet. Bernard walked with Ikuko to her room. They stood outside while she looked for her key. Then, for a moment, they looked at one another. She remembered how he had held her as the van had crashed into them. 'Thank you, Bernard,' she said.

'Will you be all right now?' he asked.

'Yes,' said Ikuko. 'Yes, thanks.' She went into her room. She listened to Bernard's steps as he walked away and then sat on her bed for a time. 'Maybe I should phone Hiroshi,' she thought. Then she remembered Bernard had her phone.

She decided to have a bath and lay for a long time in the hot water. It wasn't until she was putting her clothes back on that she realised something was missing. The ring wasn't on her finger. 'Maybe I lost it when we crashed,' she thought. But it didn't seem to matter.

She sat in her room, thinking about the day, wondering about Mike. She still felt shaky. Then there were steps outside and a knock on the door. She opened it. Bernard stood there, holding her mobile phone. He gave it back to her. 'I rang the hospital about Mike. They said he's awake now and he seems OK. He's going to have to stay in a few days, but he's going to be all right.'

Suddenly Ikuko found it all too much. She turned away from the door and started to cry. Then she felt Bernard's arms round her. 'Ikuko. It's all right. It's all fine.' They stayed like that for a long time until she stopped crying. She realised that she wanted to stay like this, close to him.

He looked down at her. A silent question, a silent answer. He closed the door behind them.

Chapter 6 *Telling the truth*

The light shone brightly through the thin curtains in Ikuko's bedroom. It was Sunday morning. There was a knock on the door. Lucretia's voice called, 'Are you all right? We all heard what happened. Shall I bring you some breakfast?'

'Yes, I'm all right. I'm fine. But I don't want any breakfast, thanks.' Ikuko didn't open the door. Bernard hadn't left her room the night before and he lay next to her. Ikuko couldn't believe what had happened.

She turned to Bernard and said softly, 'I have to talk to you ... There are things I need to tell you.'

'Me, too ... I have a lot to tell you. But we have time.'

Ikuko got out of bed and pulled back her curtains. Light filled the room. The street outside was white, covered in snow. The sky was blue and the sun shone. 'Come on,' said Bernard. 'Let's go for a walk. Then we can talk.'

It was difficult to walk in the snow. Ikuko held onto Bernard's arm. The air was cold but the wind had gone. It was quiet. Only a few cars drove slowly down the road leaving black pathways in the snow.

'Bernard ... I don't know what happened to me. I've already got a boyfriend in Japan.'

'Yes, I know. Do you want to tell me about him?'

'He's called Hiroshi. We've been together for two years. He's my first real boyfriend. We're getting married later this year. But I wanted to travel first, to see new places. He didn't mind at all. He trusted me . . . '

'Have you told him anything yet?' Bernard asked.

'No,' she replied. 'I thought maybe there was nothing to tell. Until last night.'

'Ikuko, there are things I have to tell you, too.' Bernard stopped and took out a small photograph from his wallet. He passed it to Ikuko. Two African children with round eyes and serious faces stared out of it. Ikuko looked at the photo and then at Bernard. She didn't say anything.

After a minute, Bernard said, 'This is Beatrice. She's eleven. Chiole is five.' He pointed to each girl as he spoke.

Finally, Ikuko found the words. 'So you're married?'

'I got married twelve years ago. I was very young. We were both very young. Too young.'

'So what happened?' Ikuko asked.

'She left me. She went back to Lusaka, to the capital, where her people live, and left me and the children.'

'And . . . what happened to the children?'

'I brought them up on my own,' Bernard answered. 'It wasn't easy. My mother helped at first, but now she's getting old. So when I got the chance to study in England, I asked my wife to come back to Mungwi while I was away. Just for a year. To look after the children.'

They stood there for a minute. Ikuko wanted to ask Bernard why he hadn't told her before. But she didn't. She gave him back the photograph.

'They're lovely. Lovely children,' she said.

'Yes,' he said, as he put the photograph away, 'I miss them very much.' They started to walk again, side by side, but not touching.

'Maybe we shouldn't see each other any more,' Ikuko said. She looked down at her feet in the snow which was already changing to dirty grey water.

'I'm sorry about last night,' said Bernard.

Ikuko suddenly felt angry. 'Is that true? Are you really sorry?'

'No, Ikuko. I'm sorry I didn't explain before. I'll understand if you don't want to see me again. But I'm not sorry it happened.'

Ikuko thought about the last few weeks. Then she stopped and looked at him. 'No, I'm not sorry it happened either,' she said. 'And I still want to see you.'

Late that evening Ikuko sat alone in her room, holding her mobile phone. She took a deep breath and pressed the memory button. Hiroshi's number.

It was morning in Japan. Hiroshi was just getting up. It wasn't an easy conversation. She told him about the accident first.

'I was nearly thrown out of my seat. But the person sitting next to me, Bernard, he saved me.'

'Bernard? Is he English?' Hiroshi asked quickly.

She had forgotten how well Hiroshi knew her. How he could tell at once when something was important to her.

'No, he's Zambian,' Ikuko answered.

'What?' said Hiroshi.

'From Africa.'

'And he's your boyfriend? Tell me.'

'Yes,' Ikuko said slowly. 'Yes, I suppose so. I don't really know what's going to happen. I'm so sorry, Hiroshi.'

She had never seen Hiroshi angry, but she could tell he was angry now. 'You promised. I've waited for you,' he shouted. 'But I knew something was happening. I knew you weren't the same. What am I supposed to do now?'

'Oh, Hiroshi. I'm sorry. I'm sorry.' But he'd rung off.

She sat there for a moment not knowing what to do. Then she got out her diary. Maybe if she wrote everything down she'd feel clearer. She took out her pen and started. An hour later she was still writing.

I don't understand how I feel about Bernard, but ever since I met him it's felt like a door opening – so many new ideas, new experiences. We're so happy together. I feel very bad about Hiroshi. But I can't help it. I thought I loved him. I trusted him, and he trusted me. But he wants a quiet life, a safe life, at home in Japan. I don't think I can live that life. Not yet, anyway. I don't know what will happen, but I'm happy I came to England.

Chapter 7   *News from Zambia*

It was a windy Sunday afternoon at the end of March. Bernard and Ikuko were sitting in Bernard's room. Ikuko was reading an English newspaper, sometimes stopping to look words up in her dictionary. Bernard was writing an essay and there were books and papers all over the floor. A CD was playing, the music filling the room and going through the open window into the spring air.

Japan seemed a long way from this room filled with African music. Ikuko had written to Hiroshi to try to explain more about what had happened. After a while she'd received a letter back from him.

I still think of you and hope you won't get hurt. I wish you'd come back to Japan. Then we could talk about this properly. But in the end you have to decide what you want.

There was a knock on the door. 'Come in,' called Bernard. Lucretia put her head round the door. 'Hello. There's a fax for you, Bernard. It was at reception. I brought it up. Here.' She handed him the paper and then left.

Bernard read the few handwritten lines. Then he looked up, his face serious. 'It's from Beatrice. My wife has gone back to Lusaka. She's left Beatrice and Chiole on their own.'

He was silent for a minute, thinking. Then he went on:

'Ikuko, I have to go back. They're too young to look after themselves. My mother and father are old and ill. There's no-one else.'

'What about your course . . . and us?' Ikuko asked.

'I don't know. But Ikuko, this can't be the end for us. We have to see each other again. But I don't know how.'

Three days later, Ikuko stood with Bernard at Heathrow Airport. Ikuko remembered the last time she had said goodbye in an airport – in Japan. What had happened to the promises she'd made Hiroshi then? She'd meant them at the time. She shivered, feeling suddenly cold. Bernard put his arm round her.

'I'll fax you as soon as I arrive in Mungwi,' he said. 'The phone's not so good for international calls. And you've got my school address – you can always write to me there. Remember, Ikuko, we'll be together again soon, somewhere.' For the last time Ikuko felt Bernard's arms round her.

'I'll see you soon,' she managed to say. And watched as his red jacket disappeared.

*   *   *

4 May 2000

Just a month since Bernard left. And still no news. Nothing. No letter, no fax, no phone call. I can't believe that he doesn't care, that he's forgotten me. I can't forget him.

Ikuko sat alone in her room looking out of the window. The trees were green now, not a fresh new green but already looking dark. There was nothing else to write. She'd done nothing special that day. Gone to classes but not learnt anything. She knew her teachers and friends were worried about her. In the last month she'd slept badly. Her face looked thin and even paler than usual. She'd written to Hiroshi – a short letter telling him that Bernard had gone home, but not saying any more than that.

She'd tried to fax Bernard, but the number he'd given her didn't work. And she'd sent letter after letter, but there was no reply. She lay awake at night for hours thinking the same thoughts over and over again. 'Was I really stupid? Didn't I mean anything to him? Maybe he's back with his wife. Or with someone else. But why hasn't he told me?'

Then the mobile phone on the desk beside her rang. She picked it up, her heart racing.

'Ikuko. How are you?' It was Hiroshi.

'I'm all right. How are you? Did you get my letter?'

'Yes.' He paused. 'So what are you doing now?'

'Studying . . . nothing much,' Ikuko answered.

'Are you still planning to stay until July?' Hiroshi asked.

'I don't know. I haven't thought about it,' she said.

'Ikuko – come back to Japan. Come back here. I'll meet you at the airport. It would be better . . . '

'Maybe you're right. I'll think about it. Thanks, Hiroshi.' She put down her phone slowly. It had been good to talk to him, good to talk in her own language to someone who knew the old Ikuko. Maybe he was right. Maybe it was time to go home.

She opened her wardrobe and pulled out the blue suitcase.

Chapter 8   *Waiting*

Ikuko and Hiroshi walked slowly together beneath the cherry trees in the park at Ome. The trees had finished flowering and it was already summer. Ikuko had been back a month, but she and Hiroshi were still careful with each other. She knew she had hurt him badly and that he wasn't sure what to do. Ikuko hadn't talked about her feelings for Bernard, and Hiroshi hadn't asked her any questions.

'Would you like to stop here?' asked Hiroshi. There was an empty seat under a tree. The Sunday afternoon crowds filled the park. Next to them, a young couple sat with their baby. She saw Hiroshi watching the baby, his hair falling over his eyes as usual. He would be such a good father, she thought. And she couldn't expect him to wait for her until she decided on her own feelings.

She wasn't even sure how she felt any more. She still couldn't forget Bernard. She had almost stopped expecting to hear from him, but part of her couldn't stop hoping. She had left her address at the hostel, and every morning she waited for the post to arrive. But there was no letter from England or from Zambia.

The next morning Ikuko lay in bed trying to make herself get up. 'But what for?' she thought. She had nothing to do that day. Except look for a job – and she knew she wouldn't do that.

She went and made herself a cup of coffee and sat drinking it. Then the post arrived. One letter. A letter in an airmail envelope. With Zambian stamps. A letter addressed to her in Birmingham and readdressed to Japan.

She sat and looked at the envelope, turning it over and over. She wondered what she expected to find inside. She opened it and started to read.

Dear Ikuko

I've just received a letter from you although I don't think it was your first letter. It took a long time to arrive. They had sent it to the wrong school, and no-one sent it on. And the fax at school is broken. We're waiting for a new part but it hasn't come yet. They say it should arrive by the end of the month, then you can fax me.

I've written to you many times, but I don't think you've received my letters either. I gave the letters to a driver to post in Lusaka so that they'd get to you more quickly. But maybe he didn't post them. So now I'll post my letters from Mungwi.

It is a good thing I came back. The children were staying with my parents, but my mother was very ill and two weeks after I came back she died. It has been a very sad time for all of us. Now I can't leave the children. I can't come back to England. My wife has met someone else and she wants to divorce me. But it will take time.

Ikuko, I left in such a hurry. Maybe now you're tired of waiting for me. Soon you'll be going back to Japan. Maybe it would be better for you to forget about me. Maybe it's better for you to marry someone from your own country, instead of being with a man who can't marry you yet, who lives such a different life.

But I'm missing you very much. I can't leave Zambia – but can you come here? I don't know if this life would ever be possible for you, but when I sit with the children in the evening, I wish you were here with us. Please, if you still want to see me, if there's any chance, try to come to Zambia. Please come. I'll be here.

Love from
Bernard

She looked at the date at the top of the letter: 10 May. The day she'd left England. It was nearly three months since she'd seen Bernard.

She found a sheet of paper and started to write a fax.

Chapter 9 *African sunshine, African rain*

A chicken hurried across the ground as a young Zambian girl in school clothes, carrying a bag of books, walked into the back yard. It was nearly five o'clock, but the September sun was still hot, shining on the cooking pots and pans left out to dry. At the far end of the yard there was a big mango tree with wide green leaves and small green fruit. The girl walked towards the back door and dropped her bag on the table just outside it. The house had just one floor, with the door in the middle and a window on each side.

'Ikuko, I'm home!' the girl called.

Ikuko came out into the hot sun. She looked very different from the pale unhappy girl who had opened Bernard's letter months earlier. Her face was relaxed and happy. Holding onto her other hand was a little girl with dark skin and wide eyes.

'Hello, Beatrice. How was school?' Ikuko asked.

'It was good,' Beatrice replied in English. Then Beatrice and the little girl spoke for a minute in Bemba, their own language. She turned to Ikuko again. 'Chiole says that today you went to the market. And you bought some tomatoes and onions.'

Ikuko laughed. 'Yes, she helped me choose them. Good ones!'

'Is my father back yet?' Beatrice asked.

'No, he's at his photography business. He'll be back soon, then we'll have dinner,' said Ikuko.

'What's for dinner?'

'Chicken and *nshima*. And salad,' answered Ikuko.

'I can make the *nshima* if you want,' said Beatrice. 'It's difficult for you. I can't imagine how you can live in Japan without eating *nshima*.'

Ikuko just smiled. She didn't want to tell Beatrice that she found it difficult to eat the heavy *nshima*. Flour and water cooked in a pan over the fire. But the children loved it and so did Bernard.

She had been in Zambia for almost four weeks. In some ways they had been the happiest weeks of her life. She had arrived at the small airport feeling frightened. Would she even recognise him? What would she do if he wasn't there to meet her? But he was there, smiling his crooked smile, looking just the same – except that in the hot sun he didn't need the red jacket. He had borrowed a friend's car and they drove from the airport to his house down the narrow roads, between low hills and trees. Everything was dry and dusty.

'Wait until the rains come next month,' Bernard said. 'Everything will be green. The grass will be higher than the houses.' Ikuko couldn't imagine rain as she looked up at the blue sky. So much space, she thought. The sky seemed wider than anywhere else she'd been.

They arrived at a square house. The two children came shyly out to meet them. Little Chiole just stood and stared with her thumb in her mouth. 'She doesn't know much English yet,' said Bernard.

Four weeks later, Ikuko and Chiole still couldn't say much to each other. But the little girl seemed to trust her. They spent a lot of time together while Bernard and

Beatrice were at school. Ikuko found that all the housework took a long time – cleaning and cooking, washing and ironing. The house had electric light, there was a fridge and a television, but no washing machine or electric cooker.

Every day she walked to the market with Chiole and bought vegetables. It was a long walk there and back in the hot sun, carrying the heavy bag of vegetables. She watched the African women with their babies on their backs and their shopping on their heads. It looked easy, but Ikuko had tried and couldn't do it. When they got back she was hot and tired. Then it was good to sit on the seat by the back door watching Chiole play in the garden.

She was always happy when Bernard arrived home, although often it was very late. He had started up his photography business, so he went straight there after school. It was doing well and he had a lot of work to do in the evenings. But eventually he would arrive, and they would all eat outside together in the cool evening air, with the sound of the insects in the dark and the stars shining above, before the children went sleepily to bed.

They hadn't made any decisions about the future yet. 'Wait and see,' said Bernard. 'Zambia isn't like England or Japan. I'd like you to stay, but you must decide for yourself.'

All through the next week it got hotter and hotter. The daily walk to the market was even more tiring. Little Chiole lay on her bed most of the day. Everyone seemed hot and tired.

'It's a difficult time, the end of the hot season,' said Bernard. 'It'll be better when the rains come.'

And the next afternoon the rains came. First the wind

arrived, blowing the dust across the yard. Then big drops of water landed on the hot dry ground. The smell was wonderful and Chiole ran about laughing and shouting.

By evening it was still raining and the yard outside was wet and muddy. Beatrice and Bernard came home with their clothes wet through. 'It's early for the rains,' said Bernard. 'It'll probably not last long. But it's good to be cool again.'

The next morning was fine, but in the afternoon the rain started again. That evening Ikuko found that the little house seemed to be full of wet clothes and muddy children. She realised how much of their life they usually lived outside, at the big table by the back door. Now they ate their dinner indoors without speaking – it was difficult to talk with the noise of the rain and thunder. Suddenly there was a bang and all the lights went out. 'Don't worry,' said Bernard. 'It's just an electricity cut. Beatrice, get the candles and then go to bed.'

Bernard and Ikuko sat without speaking in the candlelight as the storm went away. But it wasn't an easy silence. It was the silence of two people trying to decide what to say to each other.

Then Ikuko spoke. 'Bernard, I love you very much. And I love your children, too. I'd like to stay here. But I don't know if I can.'

'I know, Ikuko. I wanted you to come here, to see what it was like. But I know it isn't an easy life for you.'

'I don't think it's that. It's been a bit difficult since the rains came, but it's not that. But, Bernard, wherever I am I want to be somewhere else. What's wrong with me? Why can't I be happy with what I've got?'

'You're looking for something, Ikuko. But you don't know what. Maybe you'll find it back in Japan after all. In your own country.'

'But if I leave who will look after the children?'

'I'll have to manage,' said Bernard. 'It won't be easy, but I can do it. That's not the problem. The problem is losing you. I hoped we'd stay together. But Mungwi isn't Tokyo. I couldn't live all my life in Birmingham, even though I loved it. And I don't think you can live in Mungwi, even though you've tried so hard.'

Their conversation continued as the candle burnt down. At last the rain stopped. 'Let's go and sit outside on the bench,' said Bernard. They went out and sat on the wooden seat by the back door. The clouds had gone and the big African moon was full and bright. Ikuko reached out and took Bernard's hand.

'I think I have to go. I think in the end I belong in Japan. But a part of me will always be here. And I'm happy I came. I'm happy I have these memories of our time together. Maybe we'll never meet again, but in a way we'll always be together because we'll both remember these times.'

*   *   *

It had rained that morning, but now the sun shone on the pools of water in the yard. Ikuko sat on the bench outside the house with her blue suitcase next to her. Beatrice and Chiole were outside at the front, waiting for Bernard's friend to arrive with the car.

Bernard came out through the back door. He stood

there, looking at her. 'Stay there a minute,' he said, and went inside. He came back with his camera. The Japanese girl looked back at him, unsmiling, as the camera clicked and recorded that second for the years to come.

Part 2   Coming home

Chapter 10   *Plane to Egypt*

The hot Egyptian sun shone down on the new Red Sea Research and Tourist Centre. It shone on the low white buildings, the blue sea next to them and the green air-taxi park. It was the year 2050. Tiny air-taxis, looking like insects in the sky, flew here and there, taking passengers to beaches along the coast or to the airport at Marsa Alam.

In the research centre, a well-dressed woman with a young face and white hair was talking to a screen on the wall. She looked Arabic, but her English had no accent.

'OK, Joyce. Well, as you know, the opening ceremony begins at eleven o'clock and your presentation will follow the President's talk. So, we'll see you in an hour? Good. Fine. Bye, then.' The screen went black and the woman turned round.

On the other side of the room two men looked up from the papers they'd been studying.

'Was that Joyce Mutanga?' asked Sven, the taller of the two. He had very blond hair and a Swedish accent. 'She doesn't believe in arriving early, does she, Fatima?'

Fatima was calm as always. 'She called to say they've just arrived at Marsa Alam, so she'll be here in ten minutes.'

The second man looked annoyed. He was Japanese, with

a pointed chin and his hair long above his dark eyes but, like the others, he spoke in English. 'Nice of her to let us know,' he said crossly. 'Just an hour before the opening. Why on earth didn't she call earlier?'

Fatima laughed. 'You never know with Joyce, Taka. It's no good getting cross. She's just like that. But I'm pleased she agreed to speak. I don't think this centre would be here if she hadn't done so much to let people know about the type of research we're doing. She's really an excellent media-scientist, one of the best in the world, even if you don't like her as a person.'

'I'm looking forward to meeting her,' said Sven. 'She's African, isn't she?'

'I think so – though I don't know if she's ever actually lived in Africa,' replied Fatima 'She lives in Australia now, in Sydney. I think she's spent most of her life there.'

'She sounds amazing,' said Sven. 'Those presentations of hers are so beautiful, you don't realise how much research has gone into them. And she's only ... what? Thirty?'

'Twenty-nine,' said Fatima. 'Yes, you're right, Sven, she's brilliant – she lives for the sea and for her filming. It's strange though. She knows how to talk to people through her films, but when you meet her she's actually very hard to talk to. She doesn't seem interested in people at all.'

The Japanese man still looked cross. 'I met her last year in the south of Japan in the Ryūkyū Islands when I worked there. She came down to do some underwater filming. We were looking forward to meeting her. We arranged a party for her, but she only stayed ten minutes. We hardly saw her the whole time she was with us. She just went off on her own – didn't really talk to anyone. I remember her ... Beautiful but selfish, I thought. Cold.' He shook his head at the memory.

'Well, I'm happy she's here – cold or not,' said Fatima.

As the supersonic plane landed at Marsa Alam, Joyce Mutanga turned off the video-disk that she wore round her neck and stretched out her long brown legs. She would be happy to get out of the plane, but she wasn't looking forward to the next few hours.

She'd agreed to speak at the opening ceremony because she was interested in the work that Fatima and her team were doing. But even though she had worked in media all her life, she'd never got used to the public. She didn't mind doing the presentation – talking to the hundreds of people in front of her and the millions watching her on TV. She knew she could talk confidently about her work. It was what came before and after that she didn't enjoy. Being polite to people she didn't know, people who only wanted to talk to her because she was famous. Never mind. It would soon be over. The next day she'd be on her way back to Sydney.

She made her way off the plane and straight to the air-taxi. Back in Africa, she thought, looking down at the dry land. But a long way from home.

Joyce's name was known by people all over the world who were interested in studying the life of the seas. But she'd been born in the middle of Africa, in a country which had no coast, where fish were things found in the freezer in supermarkets or sold dried in the markets. As a small child she used to go to the market with her mother and father when they were all still living together, and her mother used to buy the tiny dried fish for dinner. But she'd never seen fish alive and swimming. She'd never seen the sea.

But then everything changed. Her mother moved to Australia to start a new life and, at the age of eight, Joyce joined her. She stood on the beach at Sydney, her African life behind her, and watched the waves crashing on the sand.

'I want to go in,' she'd said to her mother. Her mother had just laughed. But Joyce's school had a swimming pool and in six months she was as confident in water as on land.

She soon moved from the swimming pool to the sea and when she was twelve she did her first underwater dive. A new artificial gill, which allowed divers to take oxygen from the water instead of from a heavy scuba-tank, was just being introduced. Joyce was excited by the freedom it gave her to discover an underwater world where fish were not frozen or dried, but alive and in their own place.

'It's like flying,' she said to her mother. 'You've got no weight. You're completely free. And on your own.'

She started to make videos of what she saw, using a cheap underwater camera. Back at home, she used her computer to add words and music. Her mother worried about her. 'You're fifteen,' she said. 'You should be enjoying yourself. Going to parties. Making friends.'

But Joyce didn't like parties and didn't seem to need friends. By the time she was eighteen, and ready to begin her course in Media and Maritime Studies at the University of Sydney, she was already well known. Her work was on the Internet and she was in touch with marine scientists all over the world. She had found something that filled her life and that she was good at. It was all she wanted, she thought.

Chapter 11 *Swimming alone*

For the audience in the big central hall, it was like being deep under the sea, moving through blue waters. Wherever they looked – the walls, the floor, the ceiling – seemed to be water. Joyce's voice spoke softly, but clearly, over the music. 'And that's why I believe that this project is only a beginning. We must understand that the plants and fish of the sea live with us, not for us. We must work to make sure that we never lose this richness and beauty.'

As Joyce ended her presentation, the water disappeared and the walls and ceiling became white again. For a moment there was silence, then the room was filled with the sound of applause. Of all the presentations, this would be the one everyone would remember. Joyce stood, waiting for the applause to stop. She smiled once and then her face was serious again.

Sven whispered, 'That was wonderful. Brilliant.'

Taka nodded. 'Yes,' he said, pushing the dark hair out of his eyes. 'Not bad at all.'

Joyce was certainly a good speaker. Taka watched her step down from the platform and move towards the door.

'Come on, Sven,' Taka said.

Sven and Taka followed the crowd towards the reception hall, which was built out into the sea. One wall was completely made of glass and beyond it tiny fish swam between pieces of pink and orange coral. Joyce stood among a group of people. She wasn't saying much and she didn't look happy. Sven walked straight up to her.

'Hello. I'm Sven Berger from Sweden,' he said. 'I'm one of the team here in the Red Sea Centre. Can I just say how much I enjoyed your presentation and how much I like your work.'

Joyce looked back at him, unsmiling. 'Thank you.' She didn't say any more.

'Are you staying here long?' Sven continued. 'I've been trying to develop a new type of underwater film. I wanted to ask your opinion about it.'

'No,' said Joyce. 'No, I don't think I'll have time.' Sven realised she wasn't looking at him at all, but looking over his shoulder. The silence became difficult and he felt better when he saw Taka coming towards them.

'Hello. I'm Taka,' he said, smiling politely at Joyce. 'I believe we've met before.'

'Have we?' she asked.

'When you came to the Ryūkyū Islands last year.'

'Oh,' she replied. 'I'm afraid I don't remember you. Anyway, if you'll excuse me, I have to go now.' She turned and walked away towards the door.

Taka and Sven looked at one another, their eyebrows raised. 'She might be a famous media-scientist, but it's time she learned to be polite,' said Taka angrily.

'Cool it, Taka. She's not interested in anyone except herself. And her work. So what? Come on, let's get a drink. We're supposed to be having a good time.'

Joyce left the room, trying to keep her face calm. She knew she'd made that Japanese man angry. But why should she remember everyone she met? She was introduced to so many people all over the world. And she never could remember faces. Or names. Except the names of fish.

She went back to her hotel next to the Centre but she couldn't relax. It was four o'clock and she had all the evening ahead of her. She wondered if she could leave now. But it would be sad to go without taking a look at the sea. She changed into her swimming things, put on a skirt, picked up her artificial gill and left the room.

She was just passing reception when she heard her name. 'Joyce! Hi . . . are you going out?'

It was Fatima. Joyce didn't know what to say. She didn't want Fatima to come with her.

'I thought I'd go for a walk,' she said at last.

'Is that your gill? Were you hoping for a swim?' asked Fatima.

'Yes . . . maybe a quick one. Is there anywhere near here swimmers can go?'

'There's a beach just down the coast the project people use. I'll fly you down in the micro-plane if you want.'

'I don't want to be any trouble. You must be busy,' said Joyce.

'Oh, it's no trouble. I've booked a meal for the project team at a restaurant just by the beach there – just the three of us. We were hoping you'd join us. We're meeting at seven. It won't take me a minute to drop you there now, and you can join us at the restaurant after your swim.'

Joyce seemed to have no choice. 'Thank you,' she said, and followed Fatima out of the door.

The little plane quietly landed on the sand in the middle of an empty beach.

Fatima turned to Joyce. 'I'll drop you here – this is a

good place. The restaurant's only ten minutes' walk away. It's five now, so you've got plenty of time before we meet at seven. You're happy swimming on your own?'

'Yes, thanks,' Joyce said and got out, closing the door behind her.

Joyce sat on the beach for a long time, feeling the late afternoon sun warm on her shoulders. Then, as the sun got lower, she walked down the beach, holding her gill. At the water's edge she stopped and looked down at her feet. In her hurry to leave the hotel, she'd forgotten the bag with her flippers. 'Stupid of me,' she thought. She was a strong swimmer, but it would be difficult to swim far without flippers on her feet. Well, she'd have a short swim since she was here. She had light tennis shoes on, but the beach here was clear and sandy. She decided to keep her shoes on in case there were rocks later on.

The water was warm at first around her legs, then grew cooler as the sea got deeper. She could see her white tennis shoes shining on the yellow sand under the water. When the water was deep enough, she pulled the mask down over her face, turned on her artificial gill and dived under. Suddenly, she was in a new world. The sand danced below her and the sunlight shone through the waves making patterns. Then rocks started to appear in the sand. The small coloured fish who lived among the rocks swam so close to Joyce that she could almost touch them.

Surprisingly quickly, she got to the reef and swam along slowly until she found a place where there was a break. She swam out to the edge. She guessed that the drop below her to the bottom of the sea was at least thirty metres, maybe more. But it was far less frightening than the busy reception hall full of people. She didn't go down deep, but swam along the side of the reef, pausing every now and then to look at the fish and plants that lived there.

When she realised that it was getting hard to see, she swam back up to the surface. She realised she had been down much longer than she'd thought – the sun was low over the hills. At least she wouldn't have to spend very long in the restaurant.

Without her flippers it took her a long time to swim back along the reef. By the time she reached the break in the reef it was nearly dark. She swam back towards the land, raising her head above the water now and then to check she was swimming in the right direction. The sun had gone down now, but there was still a line of light behind the hills in front of her. She couldn't see the sand beneath her, but when she put her feet down they touched the ground. She stood up to walk the last few metres to the edge of the sea. The evening wind against her wet body made her shiver.

The water was only just above her knees now. She took another step forward and almost fell as her foot hit something under the water. Then she screamed, again and again.

Chapter 12 *Stonefish*

'I thought she'd be here by now,' said Fatima.

Fatima, Sven and Taka were sitting in the restaurant together, looking out over the water. The sun had almost set and the moon was rising over the sea, round and full.

'I expect she's just gone back to the Centre without telling you,' said Taka.

'But how could she have got back? It's too far to walk,' said Fatima. She was worried. Perhaps she shouldn't have left Joyce there on her own. 'Maybe I should . . . '

Then they heard a sound from far away across the dark beach.

'What's that?' asked Sven. They heard it again. Someone was screaming. Sven and Fatima looked at one another.

'We'll take the plane,' said Fatima. 'We might need it. And it's got lights.'

But Taka was already out of his seat and running. He could only hear the sound of his own breath. He was a good runner but the sea was almost three hundred metres away and the soft sand made running difficult. But he knew that every second might count.

He had almost run past Joyce in the dark when he heard her crying. She was sitting half in and half out of the water, holding one leg.

'Joyce. What's happened?' he asked.

But she didn't seem to hear him. He bent over her and tried to lift her to her feet but she screamed. Very carefully, he picked her up in his arms and carried her a little way up the beach, then laid her down on the sand. He got down beside her. In the moonlight he could see that there was dark blood on the white shoe on her left foot. He felt the bottom of the shoe gently. There were four round holes. He suddenly felt frightened and angry.

'You've stepped on a stonefish,' he said. 'You know all about the sea, and then you go out in shoes like this. Why weren't you more careful?'

Joyce didn't reply. Her eyes were closed and her whole body was shaking. Taka took off her shoe. Her foot was already starting to get bigger and he could see the four dark marks where the sharp poisonous spines on the stonefish's back had gone deep into her foot. Taka felt her leg. The poison was already moving upwards. He spoke more to himself than to Joyce now.

'Four holes. That's a lot of poison. She could lose the leg – or worse. It needs something doing to it – fast. Where the hell are the other two?'

There was a low humming sound over by the restaurant. He looked up and saw a light coming nearer, about five metres above the ground. It landed on the soft sand a few metres away. Fatima called out of the window. 'What's the matter? What's happened?'

'It's Joyce. She's stepped on a stonefish,' said Taka. 'We need to do something for her now, then get her to hospital. Is there a medical pack in the plane?'

'Yes – under your seat, Sven – but I don't know if there's anything for stonefish.'

Sven got out, holding a red box. Taka opened it. 'Good. OK, there's some useful stuff here … If I give her this, it should do something about the poison.' He took out a small plastic bottle and checked it carefully, then opened up one end. He held the bottle against Joyce's foot and pressed a small button. She didn't move.

'That should stop the poison. Now she needs to get to hospital fast.'

He picked her up and carried her to the plane, laying her carefully in the back. There was one place left in the front. 'Do you want to come with us, Taka?' asked Fatima.

'No,' said Taka. 'You two go. I need a walk. And a drink. She'll be OK with you.'

And as the little plane disappeared in the sky Taka walked across the moonlit beach back to the restaurant. 'Why wasn't she more careful?' he asked himself again. But he felt more unhappy than angry.

Chapter 13   *White shoes*

Joyce didn't know where she was. In her mind, confused by the poison from the stonefish and the drugs, she felt as though she was back underwater, but the water was very warm. Too warm ... In fact it was almost burning her ... Or maybe she had been out in the sun too long. You had to be careful with the sun in the hot season in Africa. She needed something to drink – she was very thirsty.

'Mother!' she called. 'Father!'

They couldn't be far away. Why had they put her to bed? Joyce decided to get up. She looked down ... She was wearing her best dress, the one she had been given for her sixth birthday. And her new white shoes. But there was a problem with her shoes ... she couldn't remember what. She'd done something to them and her father was angry with her. And her foot hurt, her foot and her leg. Maybe the white shoes were hurting her.

'Father,' she heard herself crying.

She tried to get up but when she moved her leg the pain made her stop. She knew that something was wrong. She lay in the hospital bed, the sheet white against her skin, living again that last day in the small house in Zambia.

She'd gone out playing in her new white shoes. It was the rainy season and the road was muddy. She'd been playing with her friends and got red mud all over her shoes. She tried to wash them in a small pool of water by the road, but they just looked worse.

When she got home her father shouted at Joyce. 'Your new shoes! Why weren't you more careful?' And then her mother came in and started shouting at her father. They didn't notice the little girl go to her bedroom. They didn't hear her crying herself to sleep.

In the morning her father had gone to work. But her mother had packed a suitcase and the two of them had travelled all day in the bus along the muddy road, back to Mungwi and her grandfather's house. She never saw her father again.

Joyce opened her eyes and said to the doctor bending over her, 'Are you angry? About my shoes?'

'No-one's angry,' said the doctor. Joyce stared for a minute. 'Who are you? You're not my father,' she said.

'I'm a doctor. You stepped on a stonefish. You're going to be all right.' He looked at the computer screen next to her bed. 'You need to rest. I'm giving you some drugs to help you to sleep. When you wake up you'll feel better, and you can see your friends. OK?'

'No ... I don't want to see anyone,' said Joyce. She still felt confused, felt that in some way she'd behaved badly. She fell back into a restless sleep again, with the pain still there under the drugs.

When she woke up again she was on her own. The sun was shining through the window of her small private room in the hospital. The clock on her silver video screen said nine o'clock. The pain in her leg was not as bad, but she had a headache and she was very thirsty.

The door opened and a woman came in with breakfast. Joyce wasn't hungry but she drank the orange juice. The sun moved around the walls of the hospital room. She slept a little. When she woke up there was a message on the computer screen next to her bed.

'Joyce, I do hope you're all right. Is there anything we can do for you? Call me any time, Fatima.'

But she didn't want to see Fatima.

A nurse looked in but Joyce kept her eyes shut and she left. Confused memories came and went. Applause from an audience . . . a man's angry face . . . someone carrying her.

The next thing she knew there were quick steps outside in the corridor. They stopped for a moment. Then the door opened. Joyce still didn't open her eyes.

'Joyce?'

It was a voice she knew, a man's voice. She suddenly remembered the pain in the water. How someone had picked her up . . . She remembered this voice, soft but angry.

'Yes . . . I should have been careful,' she said.

She opened her eyes and saw Taka's face.

Chapter 14 *The visit*

Taka stood by the bed looking down at her lying there, her dark eyes very big in her brown face, her hands lying still on the white sheets. She suddenly looked very young to him, no longer the powerful woman who had made him so angry, but a frightened girl who had nearly died in the sea she loved.

'I'm sorry I said that,' he said. 'I thought you were going to die. I was frightened.'

Joyce closed her eyes. Taka saw two tears run down her cheeks. Without thinking, he reached out and took her hand.

'Joyce, you're OK. You're going to be fine.'

'I'm sorry. I don't know what the matter is. I've had dreams . . . ' Her voice was quiet.

'I expect they've given you drugs. To stop the pain.'

'Yes,' she said.

'That's probably what's doing it. But you should be all right now. Do you want me to call anyone?'

'No. No-one.' Joyce closed her eyes.

'Are you tired? Do you want me to go?' Taka asked.

She was still for a minute, then she shook her head. 'No,' she said softly. 'Stay here for a bit.'

For a long time Taka sat by the bed, holding her hand. He wasn't sure if she was awake or asleep. Then she said softly, still with her eyes closed. 'Taka . . . what happened?'

'It was a stonefish,' he said.

He felt her hand hold his tighter. Then she opened her eyes and looked at him. 'I would have died, wouldn't I? If you hadn't been there.'

'You could have done.' He remembered the feel of her body, shivering with pain and cold, as he'd carried her out of the dark water.

She was quiet for a moment. She moved her leg under the covers, carefully.

'Does it still hurt?' he asked.

'Yes, but it's much better than it was. How long do you think I'll have to stay here?'

'Not long. I expect you'll be swimming again in a week,' he said, trying to be cheerful.

She bit her lip. Suddenly she looked tired.

'I'd better go,' said Taka. She nodded her head and he let go of her hand. He didn't want to leave her.

'I'll come back this evening if you want,' he offered.

She smiled and said, 'Yes, I'd like that.'

Taka left the room and Joyce lay there on her own again. She thought about her dream. The memory of that day in Zambia had been hidden very deep in her mind. It had needed the pain and the drugs to bring it back. Now she lay and thought about it all, the people who had been part of her life there, and what they had meant to her.

Taka left the hospital and came out into the hot air. He went back to the research building and sat in front of his computer for a few minutes. But he couldn't work. He typed Joyce's name into the computer and called up the recording of her presentation. He replayed the last few minutes when the lights came up and Joyce's face filled the screen. He looked at her dark head and long neck, the high cheekbones, the shy, crooked smile she gave as her talk ended. Then, not knowing quite why he did it, he copied the recording onto the video-disk he wore round his neck.

He stood up and moved around the room restlessly. Just then the video-disk round his neck beeped. A call. A white-haired Japanese woman was standing in a garden. She spoke to him in Japanese. 'Taka. You're looking very well,' she said.

'Grandmother!'

'But your hair needs cutting! You're just like your grandfather. Never time for a haircut. Hair falling into your eyes.'

Taka laughed. His grandmother and he had always been very close. Taka was her first grandchild and the only boy.

'I've been busy! We've just had the opening ceremony for the Centre,' he explained.

'Do you realise how long it is since you visited me? I think it's time you came. Take the weekend off. You work too hard! I'll see you on Saturday.' And his disk went dark again as she finished speaking.

Chapter 15   *Night dive*

That evening Joyce sat by the window in her room in the hospital. She had a thin plastic covering on her left foot. She looked out at the sea in the light of the setting sun. Only twenty-four hours ago she'd been swimming in that sea, feeling safe and at home in the water. She shivered, remembering the danger that the water had hidden.

She heard quick steps coming down the corridor, almost running, then the door opened. She knew who it would be and she was smiling as she turned around. 'Taka!' she said.

'How are you feeling?' he asked.

'Oh, OK. Fine, in fact.'

'Have you seen the doctor again?'

'Yes,' replied Joyce. 'He says I'm all right. He says I can leave tonight if I want. I can walk fine. A bit slow, but it doesn't hurt at all. It's amazing, isn't it? Only twenty-four hours. He says it's because you acted so quickly.'

'Oh,' said Taka. 'That's great.' But he didn't seem sure. He paused for a minute. 'So where will you go now?'

'Home, I suppose,' said Joyce.

'Back to Sydney?' asked Taka.

Joyce thought of her tiny flat in Sydney where she stayed in between travelling. But was it her home?

'Yes, I suppose so,' she said quietly.

'Do you have family there?' Taka asked.

'No ... well, my mother used to be there but she lives in the USA now.'

Taka paused, then spoke very fast. 'Why don't you stay for a day or two. I could show you some of the work we've been doing. '

Joyce looked up at him, uncertain. 'I ... I'm not sure. Aren't you busy?'

'No, I've got some holiday to take. We could go swimming. You could stay with me.'

'No!' said Joyce, and saw Taka's eyes widen. 'Sorry, I meant ... I don't want to go in the sea.'

She didn't know how to explain to him that the thought of the sea, the dark water, filled her with fear. That she felt as if she never wanted to go back there.

Taka looked at her. 'Did the doctor say you could swim?'

'Yes ?' she said slowly.

'Right. We're going diving. Right now. You've got to get back into the sea – you've got to face this fear.'

Joyce looked out of the window. The sun had almost set. There were just lines of red in the west. 'I didn't say I was afraid.'

He looked at her. 'You didn't need to say it. I can see. I've been the same – once when my gill went wrong. The only thing to do is to face up to it straight away. But not on your own. We'll do this together.'

'But it's dark ... ' Joyce began.

'So we'll do a night dive,' Taka said as he jumped to his feet. 'Come on. Your gill's here. And I've got everything else we need. We'll tell the doctor on the way out.'

And Joyce found herself walking out of the door.

Half an hour later they were sitting in the micro-plane.

Taka turned to her, smiling. 'It's ages since I've done a night dive. I suppose you've done lots?'

'Yes ... but not for a long time.'

'We'll take a boat out to the reef. Then we can get straight to the deep water,' he said.

They landed behind the restaurant. Five minutes later they were sitting in a little boat moving quietly over the calm water. The moon was out, almost full, making a white path down the sea. In front of them a narrow line of white showed where the rocks of the reefs came up to the top of the water. Then they were through the break in the reef where she had swum the day before. Taka stopped the boat. He handed her a headband with a light on it, and put one around his own head. They put on their flippers and artificial gills.

'Ready?' he asked. Then he was over the side of the boat and in the water. The boat rocked and then was still again. Joyce put a hand over the side. The water was cold and dark. She thought of how far it went below them.

'I can't go in,' she said.

Taka looked at her from the water. 'You've got to come in, Joyce. You can do it.'

Joyce stood up. She waited a few seconds, unsure. Then, suddenly, she dived and was gone.

For a moment Taka was frightened. Then he saw a light moving up through the water towards him. Her head appeared, wet and shining.

'It's beautiful!' she said. 'Come on, Taka.' She took his hand.

Slowly they swam together, his pale body next to her dark one. The coral shone red and purple, quite different from the daytime colours. Beautiful fish came out of their homes in the reef, attracted by the lights Joyce and Taka carried. Now and then Joyce would point at something: Taka's eyes would follow her finger and see some special fish or plant.

They came to the surface together. Taka turned off his torch and leaned over to turn off Joyce's. The full moon shone over them. The lights of the restaurant could be seen in the distance. But here they were on their own.

'Cold?' he asked her. She shook her head.

'I feel wonderful,' she said, smiling. 'Thank you, Taka.'

He reached out a hand to her and pulled her towards him. She came easily, her body weightless in the water. Then he kissed her and she tasted of the sea.

*   *   *

Less than an hour later they were at the restaurant. They sat outside looking over the dark water in the moonlight, waiting for their food to arrive.

'Do you often go back to Japan?' Joyce asked Taka.

'I haven't been back for a while. But I'm going on Saturday – to see my grandmother.'

'How old is she?' Joyce asked.

'Oh ... about seventy. Not so old.'

'Are you close to her?'

'Yes ... I'm her only grandson. She always wanted me to study and travel. I don't think she had a very exciting life – high school, college, company job. Once she was married she left work to have my mother and never went back. She and my grandfather live a quiet life. She speaks good

English, though. She used to make me practise with her when I was young. I don't know how she learned it so well.'

'And your grandfather? Is he still alive?' asked Joyce.

Taka smiled. 'Yes. I'm supposed to look like him, but I can't see it. Everyone says so, though.'

'It must be nice. To be all together: parents, grandparents, children. I'd like that, I think.' Joyce looked suddenly lonely.

Taka reached out and took her hand. 'Joyce, have you thought any more about staying here? Do you have to go back to Sydney? Can't you stay a little longer?'

'Where would I stay?' she asked.

'Stay with me,' he said.

She shook her head. 'Taka,' she said, 'I . . . I'd like to. But I don't think I can.' She paused, looking for words.

'I know. It's all been so sudden. But – ' Taka began.

'No, it's not that. It's that I'm not really used to staying with people. I don't think I'm any good at it. My mother wasn't, nor was my grandmother. They both ran away. When my mother left my father, she took me up to my grandfather's house. Then she left Zambia and got a job in Australia. She left me with my grandfather.'

'Were you very unhappy?' asked Taka, thinking of the little girl left on her own.

'No . . . not then. I missed my parents at first. But I was very happy with my grandfather.'

She told him about her life in those years, walking home to the little house from the primary school down the road with her friends, the red dust warm on her feet. Sitting with her grandfather outside the house at the back, doing her homework. Climbing the mango tree when no-one was looking and eating the sweet yellow fruit.

Then the letter had come from her mother. She had a good job in Australia. She had found a school for Joyce. She wanted her back.

'I cried and cried. I didn't want to go to Australia. I didn't even know where it was. But I went. And then I found the sea. That seemed safe. It was always there.'

'Yes,' said Taka. He was beginning to understand. 'But what about your grandfather?' he asked.

'I really missed him. We used to write sometimes. Once a year or so. Paper letters. He didn't like other messages. He wouldn't use a video-disk. And I went to see him once or twice, just for a few days. But the last few years I've been so busy ... Then I had a message from my aunt ... my mother's younger sister. Just before I came here. He'd died. He was eighty.'

'I'm sorry,' said Taka.

'I hadn't even known he was ill,' Joyce continued. 'But I was thinking about him today when I was in the hospital. I think I want to go back. Just to see the place again.'

Taka was quiet for a long time. Joyce started to feel nervous. She'd never told anyone so much about herself before. She'd never met anyone she wanted to tell.

'Joyce, you must be tired. Come on. I'll take you back to your hotel,' Taka offered.

Soon afterwards they were walking into the hotel. Taka waited as Joyce went to get her room key. The receptionist gave it to her, then handed her something else. Joyce looked down at it for a minute, then came towards Taka.

'Look.' She gave it to him. It was a paper envelope, looking old and dirty as if many people had touched it. Joyce's Sydney address had been crossed out and it had been readdressed to the hotel in Egypt. On the back of the envelope there was a name and address: Bernard Chiluba, 42 Kasama Road, Mungwi, Northern Province, Zambia.

'Bernard Chiluba?'

'My grandfather. It's taken three weeks to get to me. He must have written it just before he died.'

He handed it back to her. She opened it slowly. A key fell from the envelope and dropped onto the floor. Taka bent down and picked it up. It was an old metal key. He held it while Joyce read the letter: a single page of handwriting. Then she handed the letter to him.

Dear Joyce

I wanted to write to you because I know it's time to say goodbye. I've had a long life and now I think it's been long enough. I hope that sometime you'll come back to Mungwi. My house is waiting for you. Here is a key. You'll find some boxes in your old bedroom. They're for you. Maybe you'll find something to look at there.

I hope the house will be a place where you can spend some of your time, and maybe bring your family when you have one. Your mother never found a place where she could be happy, and neither did your grandmother. I'm sorry I couldn't make a place for them. But I hope that you will find a place where you can stay, somewhere in this small world.

Love from
Grandfather

'I have to go,' said Joyce. 'I'll fly from here. I could be there by tomorrow. I'll ask about tickets now. I can fly direct to Lusaka, then change . . . '

Taka shook his head. 'Joyce, you can't do anything more tonight. You need to sleep. All this after the dive. I shouldn't have taken you out there tonight.'

She looked at him. 'I'm pleased you did.'

'I'll book your flight,' he said. 'I need to get my ticket for Japan anyway. I'll come and meet you here tomorrow morning. We can have breakfast together.'

She put her hand on his arm. 'Wait,' she said.

He stopped and looked at her, uncertain.

'If it's all right,' she continued, 'I'd like to stay with you tonight.'

Chapter 16 *A white diary*

In the end it was three days before they booked the tickets. Three days in which they spent long lazy hours in and out of the sea, returning to Taka's flat to shower off the salt and sand. They woke up late each morning, the bedroom curtains waving in the wind from the sea. They'd turned off their video-disks, letting the messages pile up with no-one to read them.

Until, on the third morning, Taka woke up and stretched, then said, 'Joyce. What day is it?'

Joyce opened her eyes. 'Does it matter?'

But Taka was already racing round the room. 'It's Friday. Grandmother. I promised her I'd be there tomorrow. Where's my video-disk? I need to get the tickets. Joyce, do you want to come with me?'

She laughed. 'No. Remember – I'm going to Mungwi.'

He stopped and came and sat on the bed next to her. 'But you'll come back? You won't just disappear? We haven't talked.'

'We've talked for three days,' she said.

'Yes, but not about what we're going to do next.'

'Don't worry,' Joyce said. 'Just book those flights.'

That evening Taka was halfway around the world on the last part of his journey. He walked down the quiet road where his grandmother lived. The house was only two floors high and more than sixty years old. Very old for Japan. He walked up to the entrance and the door opened. He heard his grandmother's voice call, 'Taka, come on in. I'm in the living room.' She sat in her low chair, her white hair around a pale face that looked younger than she was.

'So you're here,' she said as he entered the room.

Taka put his hand up and pushed the hair out of his eyes.

'Well, you're still the same. Your hair's still too long. Just like your grandfather,' she continued.

'Where is grandfather?' Taka asked.

'Out. He'll be back soon. Anyway, tell me what you've been doing. You look very well. Relaxed.'

'Yes.' He wondered how much to tell his grandmother. How much she'd understand. She probably dreamed of a nice Japanese wife for her only grandson.

'So your research centre's open now? How did the opening go?'

'It went really well. We had the President there. And a good opening presentation by a Zambian researcher. A media-scientist. She does underwater films.'

His grandmother sat up a bit straighter. 'Zambian. That's interesting,' she said. 'I'd like to have seen that.'

'Well, if you're interested, I can show you the presentation. It's recorded on my video-disk.'

He turned on the video-disk and found the recording, then handed it to his grandmother. But she didn't seem interested in the sea-life. She moved on quickly to the last part, with the close-up of Joyce speaking. She paused the recording and looked more carefully. Taka looked over her shoulder. There was Joyce looking back, with the shy crooked smile he'd seen so often in the last few days.

'She's a lovely girl,' his grandmother said. 'What's her name?'

'Joyce. Joyce Mutanga.'

His grandmother looked at him. 'Funny, a Zambian woman doing research on sea-life. Zambia's not by the sea.'

He looked at her in surprise. He didn't know his grandmother had even heard of Zambia. 'She was brought up in Sydney,' he replied.

'Oh, so you know her?' his grandmother asked.

He wasn't sure what to say. But he wanted to tell his grandmother about this new person in his life.

'Yes,' he said, 'I know her.' And he told her the story of the last five days.

'So you see,' he finished, 'she's gone back to this village, to Mungwi. To the house where she lived with her grandfather. Then she'll call me and we'll meet up. I don't know where. It doesn't matter. But I'm sure we'll meet up.'

During the story Taka's grandmother had gone very quiet. 'I'm sorry about Bernard,' she said in a low voice when Taka had finished.

Taka looked at her, confused. Who was Bernard? Then he remembered it was the name on the envelope that Joyce had shown him. The name of Joyce's grandfather. But surely he hadn't told his grandmother that?

A moment later his grandmother got up and went to a cupboard. She reached inside, right to the back, and took out a small white book. Taka noticed her hands were shaking.

'Taka, I'd like you to have this,' she said. 'It's a diary I kept for a few months many years ago, before I married your grandfather. I've never shown it to anyone. I want you to read it. And maybe Joyce would like to read it, too. Now I'm feeling a bit tired. I think it's time for my rest.'

Taka took the diary. There was a name on the outside: Ikuko Kanazawa.

'Kanazawa?' he said.

'That was my name before I was married.' She closed her eyes.

He put the diary carefully in his bag and got up. His grandmother spoke again, her eyes still closed. 'Next time you come, bring Joyce Chiluba.'

'She's Joyce Mutanga, grandmother.'

'Never mind. Joyce from Mungwi.'

Chapter 17   *A box of photographs*

Joyce stopped the taxi in Mungwi at the corner of Kasama road and got out. She wanted to make the last part of her journey on foot. She'd hardly recognised the centre of the village. Tall new buildings stood where the old market place had been, and the old school was now an Open Education Centre. But along her road things hadn't changed so much. The houses looked smaller than she remembered and the street was narrower, but she'd only been an eight-year-old girl.

It was the end of the rainy season and the road was dry. Joyce walked on to number 46. The curtains were closed. She took the metal key out of her bag and opened the front door.

She walked into the hot dark living room. Her grandfather's bedroom was off on the left, and the kitchen and her room were at the back. She opened the door into her grandfather's room. The bed was made and the curtains were closed. It was tidy, too tidy.

She shut the door quickly and went through to the room that had been hers and, before that, where her mother and aunt had slept when they were little girls. There were two narrow beds. Joyce sat on the bed that had been hers. She remembered the nights she'd lain there while her grandfather watched the old television in the living room or listened to music. No arguments, no shouting. Just her and her grandfather. She realised that here she felt at home.

Was it the only place? She thought of the sunshine coming through the windows in Taka's flat. No, now there was somewhere else, someone else. But it was still good to be here.

She sat and looked around the room. Boxes were piled up in a corner, covered in dusty plastic. She pulled the plastic back and looked at them. Some were dated. The dates went back over sixty years. Joyce picked up as many of the boxes as she could carry, took them outside and sat on the old wooden bench behind the house.

It was a long bench – when she was a child she sometimes used to lie there and sleep in the hot afternoon. The bench had been very old even then. Joyce remembered how her grandfather had mended it when it had broken. Now, twenty years later, it was broken again. But it could be mended, thought Joyce. The mango tree still stood at the end of the yard, ready for little children to climb.

She put the dusty boxes on the seat beside her and cleaned her hands on her jeans. She opened one box. It was dated 2010. It was full of photographs: colour pictures of Mungwi brides and bridegrooms from forty years ago. They would be middle-aged now. Few of them would still be here in this small town – like her family, they would be living all over Africa, all over the world.

She looked at the dates on the other boxes: 2012, 2007, 2002. One box was undated, but on it was written 'England'. She opened it carefully and took out a collection of large, black and white pictures: a girl in a church, looking at a tombstone; a girl with straight dark hair, a pointed chin and very pale skin. A Japanese girl. Then a picture of an African man, sitting on a wall in front of a big old house.

There was a sign on the wall. Oak Road. She looked carefully at the man. Who did he remind her of?

Then a small colour photograph dropped out onto the floor, face down. There was writing on the back. She picked it up and read it. Chamberlain Square, Birmingham, April 2000. Fifty years ago. She turned it over. The African man and Japanese girl were standing together in a big square. Joyce looked closer, and then she was sure. It was her grandfather, not grey, heavy and lined as she remembered him but young and slim. He had a camera in one hand and he was wearing a red jacket. His arm was round the dark-haired young Japanese woman and their faces were shining with happiness.

Joyce looked back in the box. In the bottom there was one more black and white photograph. Joyce picked it up. It was the Japanese girl, but this time she was wearing summer clothes and sitting on a bench outside a house. Was the girl looking older? It was hard to tell. The pointed chin and dark eyes were the same, but in this picture her eyes were not laughing. For a moment Joyce felt as though they were looking at her. The girl was sitting on a wooden bench which looked almost new. On the ground in front of her there was a suitcase.

Joyce turned to look at the bench she sat on. It was the same bench that the girl in the photograph was sitting on. The window behind it was the window of her grandfather's house. So the Japanese girl had been here. And her grandfather had been to England. He'd never told her about any journey to England or any visitor from Japan. She wondered who the girl was, how they'd met and why they'd parted. She wondered if she'd ever know the full story.

She sat there for a time in the sun. Then she picked up her video-disk and pressed a button. She spoke softly. 'Hi. I'm in Mungwi. I'm just outside grandfather's house.' In the screen she saw a man's face, young, with dark hair falling over his eyes and a pointed chin. His eyes looked out of the screen from the other side of the world. She continued speaking. 'I've got something to show you ... but not on the video-disk. I'd like you to come here, Taka.'

'I've got something to show you too, Joyce,' he said. 'Something you have to read. And I'm already on the plane. I'm coming.'

Joyce put the photos back in the box. She'd look at the rest later. She sat and looked around her. There was a lot of work to be done on the house. It was a crazy place for them to make their home, a thousand kilometres from the sea. But a place where perhaps something had ended too soon. A place where something else could begin.